Keto Cocktails Bible

2 Books in 1: Easy Ketogenic Cocktails Recipes for Beginners to Enjoy at Home with Your Friends to Lose Weight and Burn Fat

Jenny Kern

Keto Alcohol Drinks

Easy Keto Cocktails Recipes for Beginners you Can Enjoy at Home with Your Friends to Lose Weight and Burn Fat

Jenny Kern

Table Of Contents

Introduction

Thank you for purchasing this book. So, you've had a long, tiring day at the office and are mentally and physically drained. The only thing on your mind right now is to crawl into your favorite bar, say hello to your usual bartender, and order a nice and tasty cocktail to help you kick back and unwind. For years, cocktails, those delicious alcoholic blends, have been helping tense and stressed people relax and unwind. However, how many of these drinkers know how to make them themselves? In this book we will follow you step by step to create your favorite cocktails. I hope you like them.

Enjoy.

Wine and Champagne Keto Cocktails

Lava Champagne with Gelatin

Preparation time: 10 minutes

Servings: 6

Ingredients:

1 750-ml. bottle champagne

1 c. vodka

1 c. boiling water

1 3-oz. package blue or red instant Jell-O mix

Directions:

Mix the boiling water and gelatin mix in a bowl for around two minutes or until the mixture completely dissolves.

Pour in the vodka. Pour this liquid mixture into individual portions or small paper cups. Chill in the fridge for approximately two hours or until set.

Once the gelatin mixture is set, pour the champagne into cocktail glasses. Use a fork to break up the gelatin.

Add the mixture to a glass of champagne. Stir it gradually to produce some lava action. Serve and enjoy.

Raspberry cocktail

Preparation time: 10 minutes

Servings: 4

Ingredients:

2 bottles of cold sparkling wine of excellent quality, if you like you can choose it more or less sweet

4 spoons of sugar

4 little boxes of fresh raspberries, or an equivalent quantity of frozen raspberries

Directions:

Pour the wine, which, as mentioned, must be very cold, into a decorative container, for example, a crystal or silver bowl. Pour in the sugar, and give it a stir. Add the raspberries.

Serve as an aperitif, using a silver ladle to pour in cups or flutes.

Bishop Cocktail

Preparation time: 10 minutes

Servings: 3

Ingredients:

30 milliliters orange juice

2 teaspoons runny honey

75 milliliters tawny port wine

90 milliliters boiling water

7 cloves

Directions:

Use preheated heat-proof glass. Muddle cloves in the base of the shaker. Put in boiling water and stir in honey and other ingredients. Strain into glass. Use grated nutmeg to garnish.

Orange punch

Preparation time: 30 minutes

Servings: 4

Ingredients:

4 cups of water

25oz. of sugar

3 cups of Aperol

3 untreated oranges

Directions:

To prepare the punch, wash and dry the oranges well, peel them with the help of a peeler, then keep the peel aside.

Cut fruit in half and squeeze them using a juicer, then strain the juice and put it in a large bowl.

Prepare the syrup now: in a saucepan, heat the sugar with the water, and cook everything over low heat until the sugar has completely dissolved. Meanwhile, add Aperol to the orange juice.

When ready, add the sugar syrup. Finally, add the orange peel (which you had previously kept aside) and leave to infuse for a few minutes. Serve the punch still hot.

Tips:

Store the punch in the refrigerator, closed in an airtight container, for a maximum of 3-4 days. When serving, heat it in a saucepan.

Frozen peach champagne cocktail

Preparation time: 10 minutes

Servings: 4

Ingredients:

4ml of Alize peach

1 cup ice

12ml chilled champagne

3 tablespoons powdered sugar

2 cups frozen peach slices

2 tablespoons grenadine

Directions:

Mix frozen peaches, powdered sugar, Alize peach, and ice in a blender. Blend the mixture and add champagne until it smoothens

Pour in the remaining champagne and stir it thoroughly

Place in each glass ¼ of the mixture then take a tablespoon of grenadine and add to each of the glasses. On top add the remaining peach mixture

Garnish then serve.

Basil and Pomegranate Champagne Cocktail

Preparation time: 10 minutes

Servings: 4

Ingredients:

2 fresh basil leaves

4-fl. oz. champagne

1 tbsp. pomegranate juice

Directions:

Put the basil leaves in the bottom of the champagne flute. Add the pomegranate juice.

Muddle the leaves lightly to release their flavor. Top the mixture with champagne. Serve.

Peach Blossom Champagne

Preparation time: 10 minutes

Servings: 8

Ingredients:

2/3 c. peach schnapps

5 c. orange juice

2 c. ice cubes

1 tbsp. grenadine syrup

1 ½ c. champagne, chilled

Optional ingredient: 6 peach slices

Directions:

Mix peach schnapps and orange juice in a pitcher. Place in your fridge for around thirty minutes or until chilled.

Pour a half-cup of the mixture into 6 glasses. Add around two to three ice cubes into each glass.

Add three to four tablespoons of champagne per glass. Drizzle a half teaspoon of the grenadine syrup into each glass. Do not stir. If you are using peach slices, garnish each drink with one slice. Serve.

Gin Keto Cocktails

Orange juice cocktail

Preparation time: 10 minutes

Servings: 6

Ingredients:

4 cups of Prosecco or Spumante Brut

1/2 cup of gin

1/2 cup of natural orange juice from fresh oranges

2 teaspoons of sugar (optional)

Directions:

Squeeze the oranges.

Divide the juice into cold cocktail glasses (preferably flute or hurricane), passing it directly through a colander.

Then add the Spumante Brut or Prosecco.

Also, add the gin in the 6 glasses, if you want - add the sugar, mix, and serve.

Tips:

You can decorate the glass with orange slices and dip a cherry in alcohol.

Champagne pink cocktail

Preparation time: 15 minutes

Servings: 2

Calories: 109 Kcal

Ingredients:

2 pieces of candied ginger

0.5oz. of sugar

2 tablespoons of fruit and ginger syrup

1 cup of very cold rosé champagne

6oz. of mixed candied fruit

2 cups of water

5 tablespoons of orange vodka

ice cubes to taste

Directions:

Prepare the fruit and ginger syrup in advance.

Bring the water to a boil, then throw in the candied fruit, ginger, and sugar.

Simmer gently for 5 minutes, then let cool.

Blend everything with a powerful mixer until a homogeneous mixture is obtained.

Pass through a sieve and refrigerate in an air-tight container until ready to use.

To prepare the cocktail, pour the vodka, the mixture obtained, and two tablespoons of syrup into a shaker filled with ice. Shake with energy.

Fill two flutes with champagne and then complete them with the contents of the shaker passed through the strainer. Serve immediately.

Devil Twister

Preparation time: 10 minutes

Servings: 2

Ingredients:

8 milliliters Fernet Branca

8 milliliters triple sec

15 milliliters cold water

15 milliliters Dubonnet Red

60 milliliters London dry gin

Directions:

Shake ingredients with ice and strain into chilled glass. Garnish using lemon zest twist.

Destiny

Preparation time: 10 minutes

Servings: 2

Ingredients:

8 milliliters lemon juice

8 milliliters sugar syrup

15 milliliters crème de cassis

15 milliliters vanilla liqueur

30 milliliters London dry gin

90 milliliters cranberry juice

6 fresh blackberries

Directions:

Muddle blackberries in the base of the shaker. Put in other ingredients, shake with ice, and strain into a glass filled with crushed ice. Garnish using mint.

Crash Impact

Preparation time: 10 minutes

Servings: 2

Ingredients:

8 milliliters triple sec

15 milliliters dry vermouth

15 milliliters sweet vermouth8 milliliters lemon juice

2 dashes bitters

60 milliliters London dry gin

Directions:

Shake ingredients with ice and strain into chilled glass. Garnish using maraschino cherry.

Country Breeze

Preparation time: 10 minutes

Servings: 2

Ingredients:

15 milliliters crème de cassis

60 milliliters London dry gin

105 milliliters apple juice

Directions:

Shake ingredients with ice and strain into ice-filled glass. Garnish using strawberries and blueberries.

Alexander Cocktail

Preparation time: 10 minutes

Servings: 2

Ingredients:

15 milliliters whipping cream

30 milliliters white crème de cacao liqueur

60 milliliters London dry gin

Directions:

Shake ingredients with ice and strain into chilled glass. Garnish using grated nutmeg.

Whiskey Keto Cocktails

Original Irish Cream

Preparation time: 15 minutes

Servings: 12

Ingredients:

1 cup heavy cream

1 (14 oz.) can sweetened condensed milk

1 2/3 cups Irish whiskey

1 tsp. instant coffee granules

2 tbsps. chocolate syrup

1 tsp. vanilla extract

1 tsp. almond extract

Directions:

Mix almond extract, vanilla extract, chocolate syrup, instant coffee, Irish whiskey, sweetened condensed milk, and heavy cream in a blender.

Blend for 20-30 seconds on the high setting.

Keep in a tightly sealed container in the fridge. Shake thoroughly before serving.

St. Michael's Irish Americano

Preparation time: 10 minutes

Servings: 2

Ingredients:

2 (1.5 fluid oz.) jiggers espresso coffee

2 (1.5 fluid oz.) jiggers Irish whiskey

1 tbsp. white sugar

1 tbsp. heavy cream

6 fluid oz. hot water

2 tbsps. whipped cream, garnish

Directions:

In your favorite mug, pour the espresso in then put in hot water, tbsp. cream, sugar, and Irish whiskey.

Use a dollop of whipped cream to garnish.

Shamrock

Preparation time: 10 minutes

Servings: 2

Ingredients:

15 milliliters cold water

15 milliliters green Chartreuse

15 milliliters green crème de menthe

45 milliliters dry vermouth

45 milliliters Irish whiskey

Directions:

Shake ingredients with ice and strain into chilled glass. Garnish using mint.

Rat Pack Manhattan

Preparation time: 10 minutes

Servings: 2

Ingredients:

15 milliliters Grand Marnier

22 milliliters dry vermouth

22 milliliters sweet vermouth

45 milliliters bourbon whiskey

3 dashes bitters

Directions:

Chill glass, add Grand Marnier, swirl to coat and then discard. Stir other ingredients with ice and strain into liqueur-coated glass. Garnish using orange zest twist and maraschino cherry.

Quebec

Preparation time: 10 minutes

Servings: 2

Ingredients:

2 dashes of orange bitters

60 milliliters Canadian whiskey

60 milliliters Dubonnet Red

Directions:

Stir ingredients and strain into chilled glass. Garnish using orange zest twist.

Tequila Cocktails

Sangrita

Preparation time: 10 minutes

Servings: 5

Ingredients:

¼ cup fresh lime juice

1 cup orange juice

2 cups tomato juice

2 teaspoons chopped onion

2 teaspoons hot sauce

2 teaspoons Worcestershire sauce

lime wedges, for serving

salt and freshly ground black pepper to taste

shot of pure agave tequila (a silver tequila is preferable because its agave bite complements the spicy sangrita)

Directions:

Mix the lime juice, onion, hot sauce, Worcestershire, and salt and pepper in a blender.

Blend until the desired smoothness is achieved.

In a pitcher, mix the mixed mixture with the orange juice and tomato juice.

Chill.

Before you serve, stir thoroughly, pour into little glasses, and pour tequila into separate shot glasses.

Drink the tequila, suck on a lime wedge, and chase it with the sangrita.

Mango Sangrita

Preparation time: 10 minutes

Servings: 2

Ingredients:

1 ounce Fresh Sour

1 ounce mango puree

1 teaspoon Tabasco

1½ ounces silver tequila

2 ounces tomato juice

Directions:

Mix all of the ingredients in a cocktail shaker with ice and stir contents.

Strain into a shot glass or martini glass.

Reverse Wind

Preparation time: 10 minutes

Servings: 2

Ingredients:

½ fresh egg white

15 milliliters maple syrup

22 milliliters lemon juice

2 dashes bitters

60 milliliters tequila

Directions:

Shake ingredients with ice and strain into chilled glass. Garnish using lemon zest twist.

Requiem Daiquiri

Preparation time: 10 minutes

Servings: 2

Ingredients:

8 milliliters navy rum

8 milliliters sugar syrup

15 milliliters lime juice

30 milliliters tequila

Directions:

Shake ingredients with ice and strain into chilled glass. Garnish using a lime wedge.

Rum Keto Cocktails

Piña colada

Preparation time: 10 minutes

Servings: 2

Ingredients:

60 ml (2 oz.) white rum

120 ml (4 oz.) pineapple juice

60 ml (2 oz.) coconut cream

Pineapple wedges, to garnish

Directions:

Process all the ingredients along with some ice in a blender, until you get a smooth texture.

Pour into a tall glass.

Garnish with some pineapple wedges.

Frozen Strawberry Daiquiri

Preparation time: 10 minutes

Servings: 6

Ingredients:

100 ml (3.4 oz.) rum

200 g (6.8 oz.) ice

500 g (17 oz.) strawberries

The juice of ½ lime

Lime slices, to garnish

1 strawberry, halved, to garnish

Directions:

Blend the strawberries until you get a creamy texture, and remove all seeds.

Put the puree into the blender with rum, lime juice, and ice.

Divide the blended mixture between 2 Martini glasses.

Garnish with lime slices and strawberry halves.

Apple Cooler

Preparation time: 5 minutes

Servings: 2

Ingredients:

2 oz. white rum

4 oz. apple juice

2 oz. Sprite

Ice

Apple, for garnish

Directions:

Fill a highball glass to the top with ice

Pour in 3 ½ oz. of apple juice and 1 ½ oz. of white rum

Top up with Sprite and stir gently

Garnish with 3 apple wedges

Vodka Keto Cocktails

Frozen special Martini

Preparation time: 10 minutes

Servings: 2

Ingredients:

1 oz. vodka

1 oz. coffee liqueur

1½ oz. espresso coffee

¼ oz. vanilla syrup

Ice

Coffee beans, for garnish

Directions:

Pour 1½ oz. of chilled espresso, ¼ oz. of vanilla syrup, 1 oz. of coffee liqueur, and 1 oz. of vodka into a shaker

Fill the shaker with ice cubes and shake

Garnish with coffee beans after straining in a chilled glass

Moscow Mule

Preparation time: 5 minutes

Servings: 2

Ingredients:

2 oz. of vodka, classic

3 oz. of beer, ginger

1/2 lime, juice only, fresh

For garnishing – 1 lime wedge, fresh

Directions:

Add the vodka, then ginger beer & lime juice to a copper cocktail mug or a highball glass.

Fill the mug or glass using crushed ice.

Stir to combine well.

Use lime wedge for garnishing and serve.

Dirty Martini

Preparation time: 10 minutes

Servings: 2

Ingredients:

6 ounces vodka

1 ounce olive brine

1 dash dry vermouth

Ice cubes

4 stuffed green olives

Directions:

Shake vodka, olive brine, and dry vermouth.

Pour into a Collins glass.

Fill with ice cubes.

Garnish with green olives.

Caramel Spiced Tea

Preparation time: 5 minutes

Servings: 2

Ingredients:

1.5 ounces Smirnoff Kissed Caramel vodka

2 ounces unsweetened strong Chai tea

1 ounce half-and-half

0.5 ounces simple syrup

Ice cubes

Directions:

Shake vodka, strong Chai tea, half-and-half, and maple syrup.

Pour into a Collins glass.

Fill with ice cubes.

Pomegranate Berry Punch

Preparation time: 5 minutes

Servings: 2

Ingredients:

1.5 ounces Smirnoff sorbet light raspberry pomegranate vodka

1 ounce cranberry juice

2 ounces cocktail ginger ale

Ice cubes

1 lime wedge

Directions:

Shake Smirnoff vodka, cranberry juice, and cocktail ginger ale

Pour into a Collins glass.

Fill with ice cubes.

Garnish with lime wedges.

Honey Cider

Preparation time: 5 minutes

Servings: 2

Ingredients:

1.5 ounces Smirnoff wild honey vodka

2.5 ounces cider

2.5 ounces apple juice

Ice cubes

Directions:

Shake Smirnoff wild honey, cider, and apple juice.

Pour into a Collins glass.

Fill with ice cubes.

Black Cherry Bloom

Preparation time: 5 minutes

Servings: 2

Ingredients:

1 ounce blood orange Juice

¾ ounce lime juice

¾ ounce agave nectar

2 ounces black cherry vodka

3 sliced strawberry

4 mint leaves

1 pinch cayenne pepper

Ice cubed

For garnishing:

2 mint leaves

1 hulled strawberry

Directions:

Shake cherry vodka, blood orange juice, lime juice, and agave nectar.

Add vodka, strawberry, mint leaves, and cayenne pepper and shake with ice cubes.

Strain into a Collins glass and garnish with mint leaves and strawberry.

Red Tart

Preparation time: 5 minutes

Servings: 2

Ingredients:

1½ ounces red berry vodka

¾ ounce black raspberry liqueur

1 ounce amaretto

½ ounce lime juice

1 ounce lemon-lime soda

Ice cubes

Directions:

Shake vodka, black raspberry liqueur, amaretto, lime juice, and lemon-lime soda.

Pour into a Collins glass.

Fill with ice cubes.

Keto Liqueurs

Benedictine Blast Cocktail

Preparation time: 10 minutes

Servings: 3

Ingredients:

8 milliliters Benedictine D.O.M. liqueur

8 milliliters white crème de cacao liqueur

½ teaspoon mezcal

22 milliliters cold water

60 milliliters tequila

Directions:

Stir ingredients with ice and strain into chilled glass.

Cold Shower

Preparation time: 10 minutes

Servings: 2

Ingredients:

Creme de menthe (1 part, green)

Club soda (4 parts)

Directions:

1. In a highball glass add ice, club soda, and the creme de menthe then stir and enjoy.

Keto Mocktails

No-Wine Baby Bellini

Preparation time: 4 minutes

Servings: 4

Ingredients:

2 ounces sparkling cider

2 ounces peach nectar

Peach slice for garnish (optional)

Directions:

Pour peach nectar into a champagne flute.

Add sparkling cider slowly.

Use peach slice to garnish, if desired.

Serve.

Orange Basil Mocktail

Preparation time: 10 minutes

Servings: 6

Ingredients:

2 cups orange juice

¼ cup freshly squeezed lemon juice

½ cup soda water

¼ cup water

2 tablespoons sugar

2-3 basil leaves

Ice cubes for serving

Orange slices for garnish

Directions:

In a pitcher, mix orange juice, lemon juice, soda water, water, sugar, and basil.

Spoon ice cubes into serving glasses and pour orange juice on top.

Garnish with orange slices and serve immediately.

Roy Rogers

Preparation time: 10 minutes

Servings: 4

Ingredients:

¼ ounce grenadine

8 ounces cola-flavored soda

1 maraschino strawberry for garnish

Directions:

Fill a tall glass with ice. Pour in grenadine.

Add cola and stir to combine.

Use maraschino strawberry for garnish and serve.

Sherbet Raspberry Mocktail

Preparation time: 10 minutes

Servings: 4

Ingredients:

2 cups Sprite

2 cups soda water

1 (12-ounce) can pink lemonade

½ cup pineapple wedges

½ cup raspberries

8 scoops of raspberry sherbet ice cream, frozen

Directions:

In a large glass bowl, mix the Sprite, soda water, lemonade, pineapple wedges, and raspberries.

Pour the drink into serving glasses and scoop one dollop of the ice cream onto each glass.

Enjoy immediately!

Strawberry Faux Daiquiri

Preparation time: 10 minutes

Servings: 4

Ingredients:

2 large strawberries

1 ½ pints orangeade

Crushed ice

1 small strawberry for garnish

Directions:

Hull strawberries.

Combine the crushed ice, strawberries, and orangeade in a blender.

Blend ingredients well. Pour in a glass.

Use strawberry for garnish.

Serve.

Tropical Fruits

Preparation time: 10 minutes

Servings: 4

Ingredients:

1 ¼ cup chopped strawberries

2 cups sparkling water

2 oranges juiced

Directions:

In a pitcher, add the strawberries and use a muddler to mash the fruits.

Pour in the sparkling water, orange juice, and cover the pitcher with plastic wrap.

Chill in the refrigerator for 2 hours.

Serve the drink in glasses.

Tuscan Fresco

Preparation time: 10 minutes

Servings: 1

Ingredients:

Ice made with filtered water

2 sprigs rosemary

1 ounce peach nectar

1 ounce white cranberry juice

½ ounce fresh orange juice

½ ounce store-bought simple syrup

1 ounce chilled club soda

Directions:

Add ice to the cocktail shaker till full.

Add a sprig of rosemary, along with the simple syrup, orange juice, cranberry juice, and peach nectar.

Shake to thoroughly combine. Strain into ice-filled glass.

Stir club soda. Use the remaining sprig of rosemary to garnish. Serve.

Mandarin Mojito Mocktail

Preparation time: 5 minutes

Servings: 3

Ingredients:

8 fluid oz of Sprite or 7UP

½ of a fluid oz of Mandarin Syrup

½ of a fluid oz of Mojito Mix

5 Mandarin orange segments

3-5 large mint leaves

1 lime

Mandarin orange segments as garnish

Directions:

Cut the lime into at least two wedges.

Place the 2 lime wedges, mint leaves & orange segments into your glass.

Muddle the ingredients.

Now place the rest of the ingredients into the glass.

Stir the drink mixture.

Add the desired amount of ice.

Use additional orange segments for garnish.

Virgin Bloody Mary with Shrimp

Preparation time: 5 minutes

Servings: 3

Ingredients:

22 oz of reduced-sodium V8

1 tsp of horseradish

1 tsp of Worcestershire sauce

1 Tbsp of lemon juice

10 dashes Tabasco

Freshly ground pepper, to taste

Ice cubes

4 cooked shrimp

Directions:

Combine the V8, Worcestershire sauce, horseradish, Tabasco, lemon juice & pepper into a glass jar.

Use the lid and shake.

Place ice into two tall glasses.

Evenly divide the drink mixture between the two glasses.

Use the two shrimp as garnish.

Keto Snacks for Happy Hour

Nutmeg Nougat

Preparation time: 30 minutes

Cooking Time: 60 minutes

Servings: 12

Ingredients:

1 Cup Heavy Cream

1 Cup Cashew Butter

1 Cup Coconut, Shredded

½ Teaspoon Nutmeg

1 Teaspoon Vanilla Extract, Pure

Stevia to Taste

Directions:

Melt your cashew butter using a double boiler, and then stir in your vanilla extract, dairy cream, nutmeg, and stevia. Make sure it's mixed well.

Remove from heat, allowing it to cool down before refrigerating it for half an hour.

Shape into balls, and coat with shredded coconut. Chill for at least two hours before serving.

Nutrition: calories 110, fat 10, fiber 1, carbs 3, protein 6

Sweet Almond Bites

Preparation time: 30 minutes

Cooking Time: 90 minutes

Servings: 12

Ingredients:

18 Ounces Butter, Grass-Fed

2 Ounces Heavy Cream

½ Cup Stevia

2/3 Cup Cocoa Powder

1 Teaspoon Vanilla Extract, Pure

4 Tablespoons Almond Butter

Directions:

Use a double boiler to melt your butter before adding in all of your remaining ingredients.

Place the mixture into molds, freezing for two hours before serving.

Lemon Fat Bombs

Preparation time: 10 minutes

Cooking Time: 50 minutes

Servings: 4

Ingredients:

1 cup of shredded coconut (dry)

1/4 cup of coconut oil

3 tbsps. of erythritol sweetener (powdered)

1 tbsps. of lemon zest

1 pinch of salt

Directions:

Add the coconut to a high-power blender. Blend until creamy for fifteen minutes. Add sweetener, coconut oil, salt, and lemon zest. Blend for two minutes. Fill small muffin cups with the coconut mixture. Chill in the refrigerator for thirty minutes.

Nutrition: calories 200, fat 8, fiber 4, carbs 8, protein 3

Thousand Island Salad Dressing

Preparation time: 5 minutes

Cooking Time: 5 minutes

Servings: 8 servings

Ingredients:

2 Tbsp. olive oil

¼ c frozen spinach, thawed.

2 T dried parsley

1 T dried dill

1 t onion powder

½ t salt

¼ t black pepper

1 c full-fat mayonnaise

¼ c full-fat sour cream

Directions:

Combine all ingredients in a small mixing bowl.

Nutrition: calories 383, fat 14, fiber 4, carbs 3, protein 8

Keto Salad Niçoise

Preparation time: 5 minutes

Cooking Time: 5 minutes

Servings: 4

Ingredients:

2 eggs

2 oz. celery root

4 oz. green beans

2 tablespoons olive oil

2 garlic cloves

4 oz. romaine lettuce

2 oz. cherry tomatoes

¼ red onion

1 can tuna

2 oz. olives

Dressing

2 tablespoons capers

¼ oz. anchovies

½ cup olive oil

½ cup mayonnaise

¼ lemon

1 tablespoon parsley

Directions:

In a bowl sauté peppers in coconut oil. In a bowl add all ingredients and mix well. Serve with dressing

Nutrition: calories 110, fat 10, fiber 1, carbs 3, protein 6

Greek Salad

Preparation time: 5 minutes

Cooking Time: 5 minutes

Servings: 4

Ingredients:

2 ripe tomatoes

¼ cucumber

¼ red onion

¼ green bell pepper

6 oz. feta cheese

8 black Greek olives

5 tablespoons olive oil

¼ tablespoon red wine vinegar

2 tsp oregano

Directions:

In a bowl add all ingredients and mix well. Serve with dressing

Nutrition: calories 383, fat 14, fiber 4, carbs 3, protein 8

Conclusion

Here we come to the end of our journey with keto cocktails. In addition to being really delicious, these cocktails will also help you lose weight and counteract some diseases. Obviously remember to drink enough water. Any ketogenic plan can cause mild or severe dehydration, which could lead to other health complications. Water also helps you lose weight, which is all the more reason to hydrate yourself throughout the day. Have the ingredients ready to make a quick drink on the go. This will help you stay on track and stick to your goals.

Low Carbs Cocktails

A Collection of Tasty Keto Friendly Alcohol Drinks Recipes from Ketogenic Margarita to Low Carbs Negroni and Old Fashioned

Jenny Kern

Introduction

Thank you for purchasing this book. In recent years, the culture of drinking has considerably evolved and cocktail enthusiasts have rapidly increased not only in number, but also and above all in the awareness of a conscious consumer to safeguard their palate and health. With this book you will learn how to make your favorite cocktails that you can enjoy alone or in company. What are you waiting for to enter the world of cocktails and make a great figure! Hope you can get passionate and become a true master.

Enjoy.

Wine and Champagne Keto Cocktails

Spanish Sparkling Cocktail

Preparation time: 10 minutes

Servings: 7

Ingredients:

Distilled water

10 clementines

½ c. sugar

1 ½ c. amontillado sherry

1 ½ c. Spanish brandy

Whole nutmeg

1 ½ cup cava or Spanish sparkling wine, chilled

Directions:

Peel two of the clementines, then separate them into segments. Fill a quart-sized container or Bundt pan with the distilled water and add in the segmented clementines to produce decorative ice blocks.

Peel the 8 remaining clementines. Mix sugar and the clementine peels in a bowl. Use a wooden spoon to muddle the peel and the sugar mixture. Continue until you notice that the oils from the clementine peels infuse into the sugar. Set the mixture aside for a minimum of ninety minutes at room temperature.

Juice the clementines until you get one cup of juice from them. Pour this juice into the sugar and peels mix. Stir the mixture until all the sugar is dissolved. Use a sieve to strain the liquid and add it to a punch bowl. Remove all the peels.

Add sherry to the bowl then pour in the brandy. Stir the mixture well.

Once done, you can unmold the ice block. Gently place it into the bowl. Add in the cava then stir the mixture gently.

Add a bit of grated nutmeg on top of the punch.

Strawberry Champagne

Preparation time: 10 minutes

Servings: 2

Ingredients:

12 ounces champagne

1 12-oz. can limeade concentrate, frozen

8 ounces tequila

12 ounces water

4 ounces strawberry liquor

Directions:

Put some ice into the pitcher then pour the limeade over it. Fill the limeade can with champagne. Make sure that the can is full and pour it into the pitcher.

Next, fill the can with tequila and strawberry liquor. Add this mixture into the pitcher.

Add water to the pitcher. Stir the mixture well. Serve with ice.

Juicy Fruit Champagne

Preparation time: 10 minutes

Servings: 2

Ingredients:

2 tbsps. pineapple juice

4 fluid-ounces orange juice

2 fluid-ounces carbonated beverage with lemon-lime flavor

4 fluid-ounces cranberry juice

¼ c. strawberries, sliced and frozen

2 fluid-ounces champagne

2 fluid-ounces apple juice

Directions:

Mix cranberry, pineapple, apple, and orange juice in a pitcher or bowl.

Add the carbonated beverage, sliced strawberries, and champagne. Let the mixture set for around 1-2 minutes to allow the strawberries to thaw.

Pour the drink into glasses then serve.

Mulled Apple Champagne Punch

Preparation time: 10 minutes

Servings: 15

Ingredients:

1 tbsp. orange zest, grated

3 tbsps. pumpkin pie spice

1 12-fluid oz. can apple juice concentrate, frozen then thawed

1 8-oz. can pineapple chunks

3-qt. Chablis wine

1 750-ml. bottle dry champagne, chill before using

1 4-oz. jar drained maraschino cherries

1 orange, slice them into round shapes

Directions:

Mix orange zest, pumpkin pie spice, and apple juice concentrate in a pan. Boil the mixture then simmer for around ten minutes. Once done, you can remove the pan from heat. Add white wine. Store in the fridge to chill overnight.

Use a coffee filter to strain the chilled wine mix. Be careful to avoid disturbing the spices that have already settled at the bottom part of the pitcher.

To prepare the ice ring, you just need to mix the maraschino cherries, orange slices, and pineapple chunks in a mold shaped like a ring. Fill the rest of the mold with water. Freeze overnight.

Unmold the ice ring, slice into pieces and add it to the punch

White Wine Citrus Sangria

Preparation time: 5 minutes

Servings: 8

Ingredients:

1 sliced navel orange, large

2 sliced lemons, fresh

2 sliced limes, fresh

1/4 cup of mint leaves, fresh

1/2 cup of vodka, citrus

2 tbsp. of nectar, agave

2 bottles of wine, dry white

Directions:

Add all ingredients to a large-sized pitcher.

Stir to combine well.

Add ice to glasses and serve.

Berry Wine Cocktail

Preparation time: 10 minutes

Servings: 2

Ingredients:

1 cup dry white wine

½ oz crème de cassis

½ cup raspberries

Directions:

Pour créme de cassis equally into each glass.

Pour white wine on top and top with raspberries.

Gin Keto Cocktails

Alaskan Martini

Preparation time: 10 minutes

Servings: 2

Ingredients:

22 milliliters yellow Chartreuse

75 milliliters London dry gin

Directions:

Stir all ingredients with ice and strain into chilled glass. Garnish using mint.

Corpse Reviver

Preparation time: 10 minutes

Servings: 2

Ingredients:

4 milliliters absinthe

22 milliliters lemon juice

22 milliliters Lillet Blanc

22 milliliters London dry gin

22 milliliters triple sec

Directions:

Shake ingredients with ice and strain into chilled glass. Garnish using lemon zest twist.

Gin Star

Preparation time: 10 minutes

Servings: 2

Ingredients:

8 milliliters sugar syrup

15 milliliters lime juice

60 milliliters gin

top with soda

Directions:

Shake the first three ingredients with ice and strain into ice-filled glass. Top with soda. Garnish with lime zest twist.

Gin Salad Dry Martini

Preparation time: 10 minutes

Servings: 2

Ingredients:

15 milliliters dry vermouth

1 dash orange bitters

75 milliliters London dry gin

Directions:

Stir ingredients with ice and strain into chilled glass. Garnish using green olives and cocktail onions.

Gin Blast

Preparation time: 10 minutes

Servings: 2

Ingredients:

15 milliliters lemon juice

30 milliliters elderflower liqueur

2 dashes lemon bitters

60 milliliters London dry gin

3 fresh basil leaves

top with tonic water

Directions:

Lightly muddle (just to bruise) basil in the base of the shaker. Put in other ingredients except for tonic, shake with ice, and strain into ice-filled glass. Top with tonic water. Garnish using lemon zest twist.

Gibson Dry Martini

Preparation time: 10 minutes

Servings: 2

Ingredients:

15 milliliters dry vermouth

75 milliliters London dry gin

Directions:

Stir ingredients with ice and strain into chilled glass. Garnish using two cocktail onions.

Rosé black tea

Preparation time: 60 minutes

Servings: 4

Ingredients:

2 sachets of orange-flavored black tea

1 orange

ice cubes

2 cups of boiling water

1 cup of Martini Rosé

orange peel to decorate

Directions:

Heat the water until it is boiling and soak the tea bags for 5 minutes. Leave to cool, then put to cool in the refrigerator for about an hour.

Meanwhile, with a pestle, pound the orange cut into small pieces in 4 glasses. Add the iced tea and divide Martini Rosé.

Stir, then add 3 ice cubes to each glass, garnish with orange zest and serve.

Whiskey Keto Cocktails

New York Flip

Preparation time: 10 minutes

Servings: 2

Ingredients:

15 milliliters sugar syrup

15 milliliters tawny port

1 fresh egg (white and yolk)

45 milliliters bourbon whiskey

Directions:

Vigorously shake ingredients with ice and strain into chilled glass. Garnish using grated nutmeg.

New York Cocktail

Preparation time: 10 minutes

Servings: 2

Ingredients:

22 milliliters apple schnapps liqueur

22 milliliters sweet vermouth

1 dash whiskey barrel-aged bitters

45 milliliters bourbon whiskey

Directions:

Stir ingredients with ice and strain into chilled glass. Garnish using maraschino cherry.

Mountain Raze

Preparation time: 10 minutes

Servings: 2

Ingredients:

8 milliliters falernum liqueur

30 milliliters cranberry juice

30 milliliters pink grapefruit juice

1 teaspoon runny honey

45 milliliters bourbon whiskey

Directions:

Stir honey with bourbon in the base of the shaker to dissolve honey. Put in other ingredients, shake with ice, and strain into chilled glass. Garnish using grapefruit zest twist.

Mississippi Punch

Preparation time: 10 minutes

Servings: 2

Ingredients:

22 milliliters Cognac V.S.O.P.

22 milliliters lemon juice

30 milliliters sugar syrup

45 milliliters bourbon whiskey

60 milliliters cold water

Directions:

Shake ingredients with ice and strain into a glass filled with crushed ice. Garnish using a lemon slice.

Mint Julep

Preparation time: 10 minutes

Servings: 2

Ingredients:

22 milliliters sugar syrup

12 fresh mint leaves

75 milliliters bourbon whiskey

3 dashes bitters

Directions:

Shake ingredients with ice, strain into a julep cup filled with crushed ice, and stir. Garnish using lemon slices and mint dusted with confectioner's sugar.

Tequila Cocktails

Tequila Sunrise

Preparation time: 10 minutes

Servings: 2

Ingredients:

50 ml (1.7 oz.) tequila

2 tbsp grenadine

1 tbsp triple sec

Ice cubes

The juice of 1 orange

The juice of ½ lemon

1 cocktail cherry

Directions:

Place the grenadine into the base of one tall glass.

Put the triple sec, tequila, fruit juices, and ice into a cocktail shaker and shake well.

Add ice cubes to the tall glass and then double strain your cocktail into it.

Serve with additional ice and garnish with a cherry on a cocktail stick.

Duke Tulip

Preparation time: 10 minutes

Servings: 2

Ingredients:

1½ oz. gold tequila

½ oz. vanilla syrup

½ oz. sugar syrup

Lemon

Orange

Raspberry

Rosemary

Ice

Directions:

Place a quarter of lemon, 2 orange wedges, a rosemary sprig into a shaker and muddle

Pour in ½ oz. of sugar syrup, ½ oz. of vanilla syrup, and 1½ oz. of gold tequila

Fill the shaker with ice cubes and shake

Finely strain into a chilled champagne saucer

Garnish with 2 raspberries on a rosemary sprig

Frozen blueberry margaritas

Preparation time: 10 minutes

Servings: 2

Ingredients:

2ml Blanco tequila

½ cup ice cubes

1 ½ ml fresh orange juice

½ cup frozen blueberries

2teaspoon agave nectar

2 teaspoon kosher salt

Small orange wedge

½ teaspoon chili powder

Directions:

Place 1 teaspoon of salt and chili powder on a plate. Take a glass and pour some orange around its rim.

Blend tequila, lime juice, agave nectar, orange juice, blueberries, and ice cubes until it smoothens.

After blending taste the mixture and add more agave nectar if the taste is harsh. Pour the combination into a glass and put some ice cubes into the glass and serve.

Paloma Cocktail

Preparation time: 5 minutes

Servings: 2

Ingredients:

2 oz. of tequila

2 oz. of grapefruit juice, fresh

2 oz. of water, sparkling

1/2 oz. of lime juice, fresh

1/4 oz. of simple syrup or agave nectar, +/- as desired

For glass rim: sea salt, coarse

For garnishing: grapefruit wedges, fresh

Directions:

Rub grapefruit wedge around the edge. Dip into salt on a small plate.

Mix tequila with sparkling water, grapefruit juice, agave nectar, and lime juice in a glass.

Fill the rest of the glass using ice. Adjust the sweetness, as desired.

Use grapefruit wedge for garnishing and serve.

Rum Keto Cocktails

Beachcomber

Preparation time: 10 minutes

Servings: 2

Ingredients:

2 oz. white rum

¾ oz. triple sec liqueur

¼ oz. Maraschino liqueur

¾ oz. lime juice

Ice

Lime wedge, for garnish

Directions:

Pour ¾ oz. of lime juice, ¾ oz. of triple sec liqueur, ¼ oz. of Maraschino liqueur, and 2 oz. of white rum into a shaker

Fill the shaker with ice cubes and shake

Garnish with a lime wedge after straining in a chilled glass

Sweetheart Sunset

Preparation time: 10 minutes

Servings: 2

Ingredients:

10 oz orange juice

2 oz pineapple juice

4 oz light rum

1 tablespoon grenadine

Lime slices, garnish

Directions:

Mix rum and orange juice, combine pineapple juice with grenadine.

Pour orange juice mixture into 2 glasses filled with ice. Slowly pour pineapple mixture on top to create an ombre effect.

Garnish with lime slices.

Cable Car

Preparation time: 5 minutes

Servings: 1

Ingredients:

1½ oz. spiced rum

1 oz. orange curacao liqueur

1 oz. lemon juice

½ oz. sugar syrup

Ice

Orange peel spiral, for garnish

Superfine sugar, for rimming

Directions:

Rim a chilled cocktail glass with sugar

Pour 1 oz. of lemon juice, ½ oz. of sugar syrup, 1 oz. of orange curacao liqueur, and 1½ oz. spiced rum into a shaker

Fill the shaker with ice cubes and shake

Strain into prepared glass

Garnish with orange peel spiral

Vodka Keto Cocktails

Perfect Pinot

Preparation time: 5 minutes

Servings: 2

Ingredients:

3 ounces cucumber vodka

1 ounce lemon juice

3 ounces Pinot Grigio wine

2 ounces lemon-lime soda

Ice cubes

4 mint leaves

Directions:

Shake vodka, lemon juice, Pinot Grigio wine, and lemon-lime soda.

Pour into a Collins glass.

Fill with ice cubes.

Garnish with mint leaves.

PinkBerry

Preparation time: 5 minutes

Servings: 2

Ingredients:

3 ounces blueberry vodka

4 ounces lemonade

Ice cubes

3 frozen blueberries

Directions:

Shake vodka and lemonade.

Pour into a Collins glass.

Fill with ice cubes.

Move blueberries to the bottom of a Collins glass.

Fruity Vodka

Preparation time: 10 minutes

Servings: 3

Ingredients:

2 ounces red berry vodka

2 ounces orange juice

2 ounces pineapple juice

1 ounce club soda

Ice cubes

Directions:

Shake red berry vodka, orange juice, pineapple juice, and club soda.

Pour into a Collins glass.

Fill with ice cubes.

Peach Melba

Preparation time: 10 minutes

Servings: 3

Ingredients:

3 ounces peach vodka

1 ounce raspberry syrup

1 scoop vanilla ice cream

Ice cubes

Directions:

Shake vodka, raspberry syrup, and ice cream.

Pour into a Collins glass.

Fill with ice cubes.

Morning Orange

Preparation time: 10 minutes

Servings: 3

Ingredients:

1½ ounces orange vodka

¼ ounce Triple Sec

1 ounce orange juice

3 ounces sweet and sour mix

Ice cubes

Directions:

Shake vodka, Triple Sec, orange juice, and sweet and sour mix.

Pour into a Collins glass.

Fill with ice cubes.

Mucho Melon

Preparation time: 10 minutes

Servings: 1

Ingredients:

1½ ounces cucumber vodka

2 ounces watermelon juice

1 ounce lime juice

4 ounces club soda

Ice cubes

Directions:

Shake vodka, watermelon juice, lime juice, and club soda.

Pour into a Collins glass.

Fill with ice cubes.

Metropolitan

Preparation time: 10 minutes

Servings: 3

Ingredients:

1½ ounces Pomegranate vodka

1 ounce pomegranate juice

1½ ounces grapefruit juice

1 ounce lime juice

Ice cubes

Directions:

Shake Pomegranate vodka, pomegranate juice, grapefruit juice, and lime juice.

Pour into a Collins glass.

Fill with ice cubes.

Ginger Beer Lemonade

Preparation time: 15 minutes

Servings: 4

Ingredients:

1 cup of sugar, granulated

1 cup of water, filtered

6 lemons, juice only, fresh

1 fresh lemon to use for garnishing

8 fl oz. of vodka

2 x 12.7-oz. bottles of beer, ginger

Directions:

Combine filtered water and sugar in a small-sized pot on high heat.

Continuously stir till sugar dissolves and liquid reaches boiling.

Remove mixture from heat. Set aside and allow to cool.

After the mixture cools, add fresh lemon juice. Stir, combining well.

Fill four glasses with ice from filtered water.

Pour 1/4 of the mixture in each iced glass.

Add 2 oz. of vodka to glasses.

Add 6 oz. of ginger beer to glasses.

Use lemon wedges to garnish. Serve.

Keto Liqueurs

Safari Juice Recipe

Preparation time: 10 minutes

Servings: 2

Ingredients:

Orange liqueur (30 ml)

Melon liqueur (30 ml)

Orange juice (140 ml)

Grenadine syrup (6 drops)

Directions:

Combine the melon and orange liqueur in a mixing glass and stir.

Add the orange juice and vigorously stir. In a chilled highball glass add ice, then pour in your drink.

Add the six grenadine drops one at a time ensuring not to stir.

Garnish with melon or orange slices.

Purple Devil Recipe

Preparation time: 10 minutes

Servings: 2

Ingredients:

Triple sec (1 part)

Orange liqueur (1 part)

Almond liqueur (1 part)

Cranberry juice

Lemon-lime soda (1 splash)

Directions:

In a cocktail shaker combine the liquors with ice.

Using a highball glass filled with ice, strain the chilled liqueur combo.

Add the cranberry juice to ¾ way up the glass and top off with lemon-lime soda.

Garnish with an orange or lime slice.

Keto Mocktails

Strawberry Basil Soda

Preparation time: 5 minutes

Servings: 3

Ingredients:

1 lb of strawberries, trimmed

The juice of a half of a lemon

½ of a Cup of loosely packed basil leaves

1 Cup of sugar

Carbonated water

Directions:

Using your knife & cutting board, trim the strawberries.

Place the berries into your blender and process until smooth.

Transfer the berries to the sieve push through using your spatula.

Toss the solids and pour the juice into your measuring cup.

Add sufficient water to fill up the cup.

Put the basil, lemon juice, and sugar into the saucepan.

Place the pan over medium heat.

Cook until boiling.

Reduce the heat and allow the mixture to simmer for five minutes.

Stir often while the mixture is cooking.

Take the pan off of the heat and set it aside to cool.

Pour the syrup mixture through the sieve into your container.

Toss solids.

Now spoon two Tbsp of the syrup into your glass.

Pour carbonated water on top & stir.

Serve and enjoy.

Lemonade Mojito Mocktail

Preparation time: 5 minutes

Servings: 3

Ingredients:

4 oz of Lemonade

4 oz of Sprite or 7UP

1 oz of mint mojito syrup

1 mint sprig

Directions:

Place enough ice in your glass to fill it halfway.

Add all of the ingredients & stir.

Use a mint sprig as garnish.

Virgin Mojitos

Preparation time: 5 minutes

Servings: 3

Ingredients:

2 Cups of water

1 & ½ of Cups of white sugar

2 Cups of chopped mint leaves, chopped

2 Cups of lime sherbet, softened

1 Cup of lime juice

1 Cup of water

8 Cups of club soda

1 Lime

Directions:

Begin by slicing the lime & chopping the mint leaves.

Now place the water & sugar into the microwavable bowl.

Place in the microwave and cook on high for five minutes.

Now the mint leaves into the water and stir.

Allow the mixture to sit for five minutes.

Run the mixture through your sieve.

Toss the leaves and set the mixture aside.

Put the sherbet, a Cup of water & lime juice into your picture.

Stir until the mixture is thoroughly combined.

Now add that mint syrup into the mixture.

Add in the club soda & stir.

This drink should be served over ice.

Use lime slices for garnish.

Coffee Ginger and Marmalade Mocktail

Preparation time: 15 minutes

Servings: 3

Ingredients:

Ginger Syrup:

1 ounce fresh ginger (peeled, and thinly sliced)

½ cup water

½ cup sugar

Mocktail:

¼ cup freshly-brewed espresso

1 tbsp ginger syrup

1 tsp Seville orange marmalade

Ice

1 orange twist (to garnish)

Directions:

For the ginger syrup: In a small pan, combine the fresh ginger with water and sugar. Simmer until the sugar entirely dissolves.

Cover with a lid and steep for 20 minutes.

Strain the syrup into a mason jar and allow it to cool.

Use as directed, and store any leftover syrup in the fridge for up to 28 days.

For the **Mocktail:** Add the espresso, ginger syrup, and marmalade to a cocktail shaker filled with ice, and shake it all about.

Strain into a coupe glass and decorate with a twist of orange.

Sherbet Spider

Preparation time: 65 minutes

Servings: 3

Ingredients:

1 cup of cranberry juice

1 cup of soda water

Fresh mint

2 cups of Greek yogurt

1 ½ cups of buttermilk

2 tablespoons of fresh lime juice–lime slices to serve

3 cups of frozen raspberries

1 cup of icing sugar

1 teaspoon of vanilla extract

Directions:

Into a saucepan over a low flame, combine raspberries, icing, vanilla, and 1 tablespoon of lime juice.

Let it cool.

Pour in buttermilk and yogurt.

Pour into a jug with a lid.

Into the freezer till frozen.

Spoon into Glasses.

Top with cranberry, lime, and soda water.

Place mint on top to serve...

Orange Mango Crush

Preparation time: 10 minutes

Servings: 3

Ingredients:

2 cups of orange juice

2 cups of mango nectar–chilled

4 scoops of lemon sorbet

2 cups of soda water–chilled

Ice

Orange slices

Directions:

In a blender, blitz orange juice and sorbet.

Pour into a jug.

Add soda and nectar.

Stir well.

Pour over ice and orange slices.

Pine banana mocktail

Preparation time: 10 minutes

Servings: 3

Ingredients:

Pineapple Pieces: 2 oz.

Bananas: 2

Sugar: 1 oz.

Pineapple Juice: 4 oz.

Sprite: 4 oz.

Ice as required

Directions:

Cut the pineapple pieces and put them in a blender jug.

Add in the banana pieces and pineapple juice.

Blend it well to make a smooth drink.

Add in sugar and blend again.

Take the serving glass and put ice in it.

Fill the glass with the drink you have made.

Top with sprite and serve.

Slushy espresso

Preparation time:1 hour 40 minutes

Servings: 3

Ingredients:

Espresso: 4 oz.

Sugar: ¾ oz.

Lemon Juice: ¼ oz.

Lemon Zest: ¼ oz.

Cream: 1 oz.

Water: 4 oz.

Directions:

Take a saucepan and add water and sugar to it.

Bring to boil.

Remove from the heat and add espresso to it.

Strain the liquid in a bowl and let it rest until cool.

Add in the lemon juice and lemon zest.

Add this liquid to a shallow dish and put it into the freezer.

Take this out every 30 minutes, crush the mixture, and put it again in the fridge. (3 cycles)

When done, put into the serving glass and garnish with cream.

White choco mocktail

Preparation time: 10 minutes

Servings: 3

Ingredients:

Passion Fruit: 2 (halved)

Peach: 1 (chopped)

Coconut Water: 4 oz.

Caster Sugar: 1 oz.

White Chocolate: 2 oz.

Vanilla Extract: ½ oz.

Coconut Cream: 1 oz.

Ice as required

Directions:

Remove the passion fruit skin and put it in a bowl. Discard the seeds.

In a blender jug, add peaches, the pulp of the fruit, coconut water, and sugar: blend well to make a smooth puree.

Take a pan and heat it super hot.

Add in chocolate, cream, and vanilla extract.

Stir and cook until the mixture is done.

Take your serving glass and add some ice to it.

Add in the puree and top with the chocolate mixture.

Serve it and enjoy.

Keto Snacks for Happy Hour

Salmon and CherryTomatoes Salad

Preparation time: 5 minutes

Cooking Time: 5 minutes

Servings: 4

Ingredients:

3 oz. smoked salmon

½ oz. leafy greens

½ oz. cherry tomatoes

½ oz. red bell peppers

½ oz. cucumber

¼ scallion

3 tablespoons mayonnaise

Directions:

In a bowl add all ingredients and mix well. Serve with dressing

Nutrition: calories 260, fat 8, fiber 2, carbs 8, protein 35

Antipasto Salad

Preparation time: 5 minutes

Cooking Time: 5 minutes

Servings: 4

Ingredients:

12 oz. romaine lettuce

3 tablespoon parsley

4 oz. mozzarella cheese

3 oz. ham

3 oz. salami

4 oz. canned artichokes

2 oz. roasted red peppers

1 oz. sun-dried tomatoes

2 tablespoons olives

½ cup basil

1 red chili pepper

¼ tablespoon salt

Directions:

In a bowl add all ingredients and mix well. Serve with dressing

Nutrition: calories 260, fat 8, fiber 2, carbs 8, protein 35

Keto Avocado and bacon Salad

Preparation time: 5 minutes

Cooking Time: 5 minutes

Servings: 4

Ingredients:

8 oz. cheese

6 oz. bacon

2 avocados

3 oz. walnuts

3 oz. arugula lettuce

Dressing

¼ lemon

¼ cup mayonnaise

¼ cup olive oil

1 tablespoon heavy cream

Directions:

In a bowl add all ingredients and mix well. Serve with dressing

Nutrition: calories 340, fat 1, fiber 2, carbs 8, protein 22

Pastrami Salad with Croutons

Preparation time: 5 minutes

Cooking Time: 15 minutes

Servings: 4

Ingredients:

1 cup mayonnaise

1 tablespoon mustard

1 shallot

1 dill pickle

6 oz. lettuce

9 oz. pastrami

4 eggs

6 low-carb parmesan croutons

Directions:

In a bowl add all ingredients and mix well. Serve with dressing.

Nutrition: calories 340, fat 1, fiber 2, carbs 8, protein 22

Keto chaffle with ice-cream

Preparation time: 5 min

Cooking Time: 5 min

Servings: 2

Ingredients:

1 egg

1/2 cup cheddar cheese, shredded

1 tbsp. Almond flour ½ tsp. Baking powder.

For serving

1/2 cup heavy cream

1 tbsp. Keto chocolate chips.

2 oz. Raspberries 2 oz. Blueberries

Directions:

Preheat your mini waffle maker according to the manufacturer's instructions. Mix chaffle ingredients in a small bowl and make 2 mini chaffles.

For an ice cream ball, mix cream and chocolate chips in a bowl and pour this mixture into 2 silicone molds.

Freeze the ice cream balls in a freezer for about 2-4 hours.

For serving, set an ice cream ball on the chaffle.

Top with berries and enjoy!

Nutrition: calories 100, fat 7, fiber 2, carbs 8, protein 6

Walnuts low-carb chaffles

Preparation time: 10 minutes

Cooking Time: 20 minutes

Servings: 4

Ingredients:

2 tbsps. Cream cheese

½ tsp almonds flour

¼ tsp. Baking powder

1 large egg

¼ cup chopped walnuts

Pinch of stevia extract powder

Directions:

Preheat your waffle maker.

Spray waffle maker with Cooking spray.

In a bowl, add cream cheese, almond flour, baking powder, egg, walnuts, and stevia.

Mix all ingredients,

Spoon walnut batter in the waffle maker and cook for about 2-3 minutes.

Let chaffles cool at room temperature before serving.

Nutrition: calories 275, fat 20, fiber 2, carbs 8, protein 20

Conclusion

Here we come to the end of our keto cocktail journey. Each unique cocktail has a specific recipe, although you can vary some ingredients to taste. You should taste every component of your drinks if you do them right. Perfect drinks are balanced between sour and sweet flavors. Outside of sweet and fruity drinks and those with chocolate, your cocktails will usually be somewhere between sweet and sour. I hope my cocktails have helped you improve your lifestyle.